Helping Your Child Stand Up to Peer Pressure

DR. KAY KUZMA

LIFEJOURNEY
BOOKS

Helping Your Child Stand Up to Peer Pressure

LifeJourney Books is an imprint of David C. Cook
Publishing Co.
David C. Cook Publishing Co., Elgin, Illinois 60120
David C. Cook Publishing Co., Weston, Ontario
Nova Distribution, Ltd., Torquay, England

Helping Your Child Stand Up to Peer Pressure
©1991 by Kay Kuzma
(This booklet consists of selected portions of *Building
Your Child's Character from the Inside Out* ©1988 by
Kay Kuzma)

Edited by Brian Reck
Cover design by Bob Fuller
First printing, 1991
Printed in the United States of America
95 94 93 92 91 5 4 3 2 1

Library of Congress Cataloging in Publication Data

Kuzma, Kay
Helping Your Child Stand Up to Peer Pressure/Kay Kuzma
    p. cm. — (Helping Families Grow series)
ISBN: 1-55513-667-2
1. Peer pressure in adolescence—United States. 2. Parent
and teenager—United States. I. Title   II. Series:
HQ799.2P44K89 1991
303.3'27—dc20   91-26513
                                       CIP

The headlines these days are disturbing. "Teens Kick Principal." Three teens walked into a junior high school and kicked the principal in the head. Why? Because the principal busted their friend so they ganged up on him.

"Four students arrested for computer info break-in." They are accused of stealing over $3000 in merchandise by using unauthorized credit card numbers. Why? Their friend Joe needed help to steal some things.

Then there's the story about a seventeen year old who stood defiantly next to a squad car after officers frisked him and yelled, "I will never let somebody punk me or tell me what I should do." Later he added, "He can't tell me to shut up. I'll shut up when I want to." When asked about his attitude problem his mother replied, "The trouble is he's hanging around with the wrong people."

Shocking behavior. But maybe not, when you realize the almost overwhelming effect that peer pressure has on kids.

Because the influence of others has a significant impact on character, children must learn how to guard themselves from unwholesome pressures and to choose friends and role models that will help them become better people.

THE IMPACT OF INFLUENCE

Teach about the impact of a positive influence, rather than preaching about negative ones. Help children to see how role models can significantly change their lives for the better. The story of Elijah and Elisha is a good example of this. Elisha was the son of a wealthy farmer. But during the three and a half years of famine in Israel, Elisha became familiar with the work and mission of God's mighty prophet, Elijah.

One day Elijah ceremoniously put his cloak, called "a mantle of service," upon

Elisha's shoulders. Elisha immediately recognized this act as a call from God that he should continue Elijah's ministry. What should he do? He saw the nomadic life Elijah had to live as he went from place to place preaching and ministering to the people. He saw how King Ahab had hated Elijah for the things Elijah had said. He knew that if he accepted Elijah's job, he would have to live a similar life and would probably never be able to enjoy the life-style of a country gentleman. But, because of the influence Elijah had on him, he chose to cast his lot with Elijah and God's mission.

Elisha became a mighty prophet of God, but he wasn't born with this power. As Elisha lived and worked with the more experienced prophet, he became like him. Elijah's faith in God became Elisha's. When the day came for Elisha to continue Elijah's work alone, he had become so like his teacher and so filled with the same Spirit that the Bible says the sons of the prophets immediately recognized his new status and bowed before him (see II Kings 2:12-15).

The Bible is filled with stories about the importance of influence, both good and bad. Lucifer's bad influence caused Eve to eat the forbidden fruit—and then Eve's influence brought Adam's fall. The positive influence of Abraham caused his household to worship God. The negative influence of friends brought the prodigal son to his ruin.

History books, too, cite examples of how certain people have influenced others' lives. When Abraham Lincoln was a poor, backcountry boy teaching himself to read, he was given a book about George Washington. The story of this great American made an impression on him. He was struck by Washington's honesty and determined to be that kind of person. The book kindled in his heart the ambition to serve his country. Later, as his political career was taking shape, he aspired to move beyond the senate to seek the presidency—to become the kind of leader George Washington had been.

Throughout history, people like Elisha and Lincoln have become outstanding individuals by following others. And today, in every walk of life, well-known men and women testify that their success came from aspiring to be like certain individuals. The more they worked with these people, read about them, studied their behavior and speech, and learned under their expert tutelage, the more they became like them.

Ask your children whom they admire. If they could exchange places with any person in the world, who would it be? Encourage your children to take a close look at their friends, teachers, and other role models. Do they have friends like Elijah who influence them to live better lives? Do they have teachers like George Washington who can inspire them to live lives of integrity? Do they have role models that exhibit character from the inside out, or do they merely look good from the outside?

OVERCOMING NEGATIVE INFLUENCES

Teach your children that they have the power to control what influences their lives and that you will help them evaluate those influences. Don't let your children con you into thinking they aren't being influenced by their associates. They are. Maybe you can't yet detect any changes in outward behavior, but remember that character comes from the inside out. The real question is, how are friends influencing your children's thinking, motives, and desires? It's worth some serious consideration.

When my son was just a preschooler, he had a playmate who occasionally used foul language. One day I said to Kevin, "Kev, do you think the bad words that Randy uses are good for you to hear?"

Kevin agreed that they were bad words.

"Then, Kevin," I challenged him, "you have to help Randy to remember not to say those words, so you won't start using them."

The next day I overheard Kevin telling Randy, "You better not use those bad words when you're around me, because I might learn to say them, and then my mommy won't let me play with you because you'll be a bad example to me."

You can't be around to protect your children from every harmful influence. You must teach them to protect themselves—to have the guts to remove themselves from bad situations. Then you must support your child by helping him to fill the void with positive influences.

Evaluate carefully your children's friends and role models. It's easy to judge the kid with a Mohawk or punk clothing as "undesirable," but don't, unless you have reasonable cause. Get to know that child. Either you will find something to warn your own child about, or you will discover a kid whose looks are a statement that he is craving attention. Maybe your family can befriend this "gem in the rough"!

Teachers, principals, pastors, and church leaders can have a powerful influence on young people. You can't expect these individuals to be perfect, but don't blindly approve of them if you begin to hear that something isn't right. Keep involved. If you observe questionable behavior, investigate.

Periodically throughout his childhood you might want to discuss the influence that friends, teachers, and others are having on your child. Here are some sample questions: What kind of an influence do you feel your friend is having on you? What positive things are you learning from your friend? What negative things? What kind of an influence are you on your friend? What type of friends do you need in order to become the kind of person you want to be?

CHOOSING FRIENDS

Making good friends is an important task of childhood. During the preschool years, parents have a fair amount of control over their child's friends, although it can be difficult at times.

Controlling neighborhood playmates is hard. If you question their influence, insist that they play at your house where you can set the rules and monitor their behavior. Even then, things can happen that you don't expect. For example, sexual play. Children are curious about their bodies, and it's not uncommon for children to satisfy their curiosity by taking a peek at each other. But some children have been abnormally stimulated, either through viewing questionable videos and X-rated cable channels, or by seeing parents or older siblings participating in sexual acts, or by being sexually abused themselves. It is very easy for these children to engage others in sexual play that is not good.

Be observant. Have an open door policy so that the doors of rooms are always left open when friends are visiting. If you discover objectionable play, don't overreact. Just calmly say, "You may not play with each other's bodies like this. Every person has private places that belong just to that person. If someone wants to see the places covered by your bathing suit, you say no. If I see you doing this again, I will not let you play together."

Friends become even more influential during the school years. That's why, as early as possible, you should encourage friendships that can have a positive impact.

Here are some suggestions for evaluating your children's friends:

1. *If you have questions about a certain friend, find out why your child is attracted to that person.* Sometimes kids are attracted to someone because of strong, but not necessarily positive, characteristics. For example, kids that seem to have power, such as the classroom bully, are often surrounded by a close group. It's not safe to be his enemy, so some children go out of their way to be his friend. Also rich kids, or those who show off their material possessions, are often more popular. But they may have a very shallow value system prizing such things as designer clothes above being kind and polite. The rebellious child is another one to be wary of. It's very easy for the rebellion of one to rub off on close associates. For example, one mother complained her eleven-year-old daughter was being influenced by a friend in school

whose mother could not control her. "I just tell my mom I don't have to listen to her. I do whatever I want and she can't stop me," was the line that her friend was feeding her. "You're crazy to do what your mom says if you don't want to!" Now, her daughter was beginning to say, "You can't make me do it!" Mom called her bluff and then had a serious talk with her about the consequence of rebellion—and the harmful influence of some friends.

2. *Watch the chemistry between your child and a selected friend.* If every time they get together there is trouble, something is wrong with this relationship. Some kids egg others on to deviant or daredevilish acts. If their time together is spent arguing and fighting, then it's not productive.

   There is always a certain amount of bantering between friends, but it should not include hostile words and actions that are intended to hurt others. If your child ignores his chores or won't do what you ask him to do when certain friends are around, he is being badly influenced by those friends.

3. *Evaluate the role models of your child's friend.* It's unfair to automatically judge a child by his parents or siblings, but you must be aware of this potentially negative influence and monitor any friendship with a child who comes from a troubled home. This is especially important if you suspect drug abuse, alcoholism, unlawful or dishonest behavior, pornography, immorality, or cultic activities. Until you can assess the extent of these activities, make your child and his friend play at your house, not his.

4. *Encourage your child to think about the characteristics he would like in a friend.* Then help him evaluate potential friends using these characteristics. Here are some traits that could be found in a good friend.

- Is spiritually sensitive or not rebellious against spiritual things. This is especially important for young, impressionable children. As teens become stronger and have established their own beliefs, they can be encouraged to reach out to unbelievers. Many testify that it was a Christian friend who led them to Christ.

- Helps your child be a better person.

- Shows an attitude of obedience toward his parents, teachers, and other authority figures.

- Exhibits healthy traits such as kindness, politeness, courtesy, honesty, cheerfulness, etc.

- Doesn't put other people down, including your child.

- Is headed in the right direction. In other words, does he have parents who encourage him to participate in after-school sports, study music or art, or take skating lessons? Does he enjoy reading, hobbies, and have chores to do at home?

5. *Open your home to your child's friends, and make it attractive so they'll want to come often.* The more they play at your place, the better you can assess whether the friendship is having a positive effect on your child. Also, if your child is having a difficult time making friends at school, having one other child over at a time helps ease the situation.

The younger the child, the more important it is that you help him find a good friend. He doesn't have to have thirty friends, but he does need one good buddy to interact with to learn the essentials of socialization!

Peers should not be allowed to undo your child's good character. He should know that if you see danger ahead with one or more of his "friends," you will protect him. You will do everything possible to limit the time he spends with that friend and encourage more positive relationships. His development and spiritual life are too valuable for you to take a chance and hope that he can withstand negative peer influence. It's just not worth the risk! And the time to make this clear is early—not during the teenage years.

In addition to all the above, children should be encouraged to seek friends from other cultural or racial groups. It's in childhood that people often develop bigoted attitudes, mostly because they have never had a close friendship with someone of another culture or race.

THE ROLE OF PARENTAL RAPPORT

A psychologist friend once commented that as a teen he had a couple of opportunities to have sex with aggressive girl-friends, but he resisted the temptation because he knew what it would do to his parents if they found out. They would be hurt. They trusted him to act honorably and he didn't want to violate their trust. In a study on why kids said no to drugs, the major reason given was, "I don't want to disappoint my parents."

Maintaining a positive relationship with

your children during the growing years is one of the most important factors in helping them resist peer influence. Every child needs acceptance. If he has received parental approval through previous years, and this is something he has grown to value, he is less likely to turn his back on this positive reinforcement when faced with a peer-imposed temptation.

But if the relationship between parents and child has been strained, and he doubts his parents' love and their interest in his life, he will have a greater need to find acceptance elsewhere. Without the restraining power of parental disappointment, peer pressure can be overwhelming.

If the parent/child relationship is characterized by conflict, misunderstanding, and hostility or if parents are controlling and overly strict, kids may rebel and choose to follow peers because they know it will hurt their parents. Once a child begins to make decisions out of rebellion, you can no longer trust those decisions. The better the relationship with your child, the stronger influence you will have on the decisions your child makes and the easier it will be for her to say no to peer pressure.

DRUG ABUSE

Kids lose control of their ability to make good decisions when they get involved with drugs. If your child is experimenting with drugs, it is essential that you get involved as early as possible and forcefully, if necessary, remove your child from this influence. Drugs can quickly destroy good character. And it's almost always peer pressure that initiates the drug habit.

Because the early stages of drug addiction are often confused with normal teenage growing pains, many parents are shocked when they learn they've been living with a drug user for a year or so and didn't even know it.

Here is the typical way that peers pull a kid into drugs. Relate this story to your early school-age kids. Warn them.

Joey was twelve. Since kindergarten, he had hung around with the same three neighborhood friends. They did everything together and were basically good kids. One day when they were just hanging around, a thirteen year old from the neighborhood came up to the boys and pulled a marijuana joint out of his pocket. The three boys couldn't believe it. They had seen the older kids smoking marijuana. They had joked about it among themselves. But they had never tried drugs. "Where did you get that?" Joey asked.

"My big brother gave it to me," he boasted. "He and his girlfriend smoke dope all the time. Sometimes they let me smoke it with them. It feels great. You guys want to try it?"

The boys looked at each other, each wondering what the other thought, while the thirteen year old struck a match and lit the joint. He inhaled and passed it on to one of the other boys while he laughed about how great he felt. One boy tried it. Joey and one other boy said no. They were afraid of getting caught. But they watched and giggled as the other two finished off the joint.

In the next few weeks, there were more and more incidents like this one. The older boy showed up with pot and one by one all the boys tried it. Even Joey eventually gave in because these were his friends. They said it was fun. And they had always done things together. At first, Joey couldn't figure out what the big deal was. He didn't feel anything—and he didn't get caught. But before many weeks, Joey was feeling it. It felt good. And still, nothing bad happened. So whenever the thirteen year old could get a joint from his brother, the boys would smoke it together. Joey was a first-stage drug user.

Most kids encounter drugs many times before they actually take the step of trying them. It usually starts in a social situation, at a party, a mall, or a video arcade, where there are lots of young people and lots of drugs. Because of their moral values, most kids are able to resist for a time, but eventually, if they keep associating with that same group, peer pressure will win out. With that first high there sets in a chemical learning sequence that makes drug users susceptible to more drugs: "When I feel bad and take drugs, drugs make me feel good." Once they've decided that, they're in trouble, because whenever they feel low, they are tempted to get rid of that bad feeling by taking drugs.

If you find any evidence that your child has been experimenting with drugs—or is associating with kids who are—don't accept any excuses. Completely remove him or her from these questionable friends and from going to places where drugs are likely to be. If you're ever going to take a stand, do it now. Don't say, "My kid wouldn't do that," because if you do, your child will most likely get further into drugs without realizing what is happening to him.

Because drugs are so destructive to character development, you must be on guard for the first signs of drug abuse. Here are the most common:

1. *Is your child beginning to dress like, look like, or talk like kids that are known to be using drugs?* This conformity may show that your child wants to be accepted by this group.

2. *Does your child often use eye drops because of red eyes?*

3. *Have things begun to disappear around the house? If you have alcoholic beverages at home, are they being used up more rapidly than usual?*

4. *Does your child sit in his room listening to loud rock music?*

5. *Does he have frequent temper tantrums where he accuses you or*

other authority figures of awful things?

6. *Has he begun to lose interest in activities (such as sports or music) that used to be important to him?*

7. *Has he begun to withdraw from former friends?*

8. *Are his grades in school dropping?*

9. *Have you found pills or marijuana in his clothing or room?* Don't accept lame excuses.

10. *Does your teen have a persistent cough, red eyes, a sore throat, and fatigue, along with extreme emotional highs and lows?*

Most parents, when they begin to see some of these things, sense something is wrong. But they don't know what, and they figure it's not bad enough to do anything about. Yet, the kid on drugs is quickly losing control of his life. And the worse he feels, the more the teen craves the self-medicated high he knows he can get with drugs. The vicious cycle can rapidly pull him down.

If you've observed any of these things in your child's life, don't waste time blaming it on growth pains. Confront your child. Don't be swayed by weak excuses. Your child may not tell the truth. He is not yet convinced he is hooked, so with a straight face he can swear he isn't on drugs. Ask straight kids who know him. They usually have inside information. If your suspicions are confirmed, seek professional help.

Your child cannot safely associate with anyone suspected of experimenting with drugs. The pressure is too strong. Your child may go to a counselor or a drug rehabilitation program, but if he comes back to the same neighborhood or school where his friends hang out, the chances are great that he will once again succumb to pressure from peers.

Peer-pressure proof your child by letting him or her know the influence that friends and role models can have on a life. When he is young and impressionable, help him choose friends that advance his character development, and keep evaluating his choices through the years. Be sure you continue to have a positive relationship with your growing child. Finally, be aware of signs that might indicate that your child is experimenting with drugs. If this happens, your influence will be greatly diminished and he will probably have lost control of his ability to choose friends that will have a positive influence on his life.

BUILD AN ACCURATE PICTURE OF GOD

A child's relationship with God will ultimately determine his character. What can parents do to help their children build a friendship with God?

I remember as a child the "mean" old ladies that lived down the block. My friends and I were sure they hated little kids, and we avoided them like the plague. As I grew by inches my concept of their meanness grew by feet. Then one day my fear was overcome by my desire to sell my quota of Campfire Girl candy, so I knocked on their door. How surprised I was when they each bought a can of candy even though they explained that they didn't like candy but wanted to help the neighborhood children! I don't know how I ever picked up a wrong impression of those ladies, but it almost caused me to miss the benefits of their friendship.

It's sad, but too often that same thing happens with our perception of God. The childhood picture that is painted for us is often so faulty that we avoid getting to know Him. When you were young, what did you think God was like? Like your dad? Your mom? A favorite uncle? How did you picture Him in your mind? Was He old or young? Rich or poor? Big or little? Black or white? Bearded or shaven? Hairy or bald?

How much of your perception of God was influenced by an artist's portrayal? Was your picture of God characterized by the serene face of Jesus in Leonardo da Vinci's *Last Supper,* or by Michelangelo's severe God of the Sistine Chapel? How do you want your children to picture God?

God is awesome to behold. Just read about some of God's encounters with men in the Old Testament, and it's frightening to think of actually meeting Him. But that's because of sin. It's our problem, not God's!

If it were in my power to paint a picture of God in my children's minds, I would want to stay away from the Sistine Chapel God, whose stern, judgmental face sends chills even through my adult heart. I want my children to see God as the Good

Shepherd looking for and loving His lost sheep. I want them to see Him as Jesus, as He said to the children, "Come to Me." I want them to see a loving, understanding, considerate, forgiving, patient heavenly Daddy. But wait a minute. Where do children get their first impressions of God? You're right—from their parents! From your life—and from mine. That's a little frightening, isn't it?

In a study of more than 10,000 children in 5th through 9th grades it was found that the kids' perception of God (religion) correlated with certain behaviors. (Merton P. Strommen and A. Irene Strommen. *Five Cries of Parents* [San Francisco: Harper and Row, 1985], pp. 137-38.) If children saw God as a liberating God who accepts them just as they are and gives them the gift of salvation, this correlated positively with high self-esteem, moral internalization, acceptance of traditional standards, achievement motivation, a positive attitude toward the church and prosocial behavior. These are attitudes and behaviors that parents want their children to have. But if children saw God, or religion, as restrictive, as stressing limits, controls, guidelines, and discipline, this view correlated with low self-esteem, sexism and racial prejudice, drug and alcohol abuse and antisocial behavior.

How can you paint a correct picture of God's character for your children?

1. *Live a Christlike life.* When you err, point out that God isn't like you; God is always loving and kind.

2. *Let your child know that God is your best friend.* Let him hear you talk to Him and talk about Him.

3. *Carefully select the Bible stories you tell your children,* especially when they are young. It is difficult to understand God's actions in some of the Bible stories that are recorded. Until your child is old enough to realize that men choose the consequences that come to them, he could get a distorted picture of God as a God who did nothing but kill people with the flood, destroy Sodom with fire, open the earth that swallowed Korah and his family, or turn Lot's wife into salt!

4. *Never threaten your child by saying God won't love him* if he's bad or that an angel is always watching him and is writing

down all the bad things he does. It's important that a child feel God loves him unconditionally, when he's bad as well as when he's good. If not, when the child makes mistakes, instead of turning to God, he will often turn away, feeling that he is so bad God couldn't possibly love him. Too many adults are struggling with this erroneous concept of God that they picked up in early childhood from naive parents who were trying to frighten their children into being good.

5. *Avoid unreasonable restrictions and rigid patterns of behavior that disregard a child's needs and wholesome interests.* One example is not allowing little girls to wear slacks, or forbidding a child to date until eighteen. If you find your child fearing you or trying to avoid you, perhaps you should talk with someone who can help you understand what is causing him to feel this way. If your child has such feelings toward you, the chances are great that they will be transferred to God.

6. *Introduce your child to people who live the love of God.* Godly persons do have an effect on children, and it may be that the

children's strongest and clearest picture of God, above and beyond their parents' example and artists' portraits, will come from godly associates of all ages.

Take advantage of missionaries and other mature Christian speakers who come to your church by offering a meal or housing so your kids can get to know these people. But never allow your children to think that people are perfect. Too many people leave a church and turn away from God because they have been led to believe that the people in the church should be flawless. When they find out there are a few hypocrites around, they use that fact as an excuse for turning their backs on God.

7. *Help your child feel that Jesus is his best friend—an older brother.* God the Father may seem distant to a child, but even toddlers can feel close to a Jesus who was born in a manger and grew up as a child. Jesus Himself said that if we know Him we will know the Father (Matthew 11:27). So, introduce your child to Jesus from his earliest years. Let Jesus come naturally into your daily conversation. For example, as you are bathing your baby

you can say, "Jesus made five fingers on your hand."

David C. Cook publishes a delightful series of books called "TUBable HUGables," which are designed to float in the water and include titles, *God Gives Me Fun Times* and *God Gives Me Good Food* These books will help make bathtime fun and bring God into your child's everyday world. Or try the "Highchair Devotionals" also from Cook. The titles *God Gave Me a Gift* and *God Is My Friend* will introduce your toddler to the Bible in a very natural way.

You can sing songs like, "Jesus Loves Me." Or try placing a picture of Jesus in your child's room, maybe one of Him with children on His lap, and point often to that picture, saying, "Jesus will always be with you." It's that first year that is the critical time for a child to establish faith in parents and his environment, and it is also the time when faith in God is most easily established. Don't let the first year slide by without introducing your child to Jesus, his very best friend.

8. *Teach your child to be open to the Holy Spirit's influence.* Although it's quite easy to teach a child about God and Jesus through the

Bible and by pointing out godly traits in friends and relatives, it is much more difficult to teach a child to know God through the influence of the Holy Spirit. The Spirit is more abstract speaking to each of us (including our children) through providential daily experiences, through our meditation, and through prayer. Speaking children should be led to understand that God's Spirit can speak most clearly to their minds when their lives are in harmony with their parents and with God—when they have nothing to hide. Indeed, when children feel good about themselves and about their behavior (when they are living a Spirit-filled life), they are eager to learn more about God.

TALK TO GOD

You can't have much of a relationship with someone if you never talk to each other. Prayer is the way we talk to God, but too often it ends up being a mere bedtime, mealtime, and church-time ritual. What our children really need is to learn how to talk with God all day long, not just when they are expected to say, "I'm sorry," "Please give me," or "Thank You."

I doubt that you would have many

friends if you only talked to them when you had done something wrong, when you needed something, or when you wanted to say thank you. Relationships grow on chitchat, brainstorming, discussing ideas and plans, telling stories and jokes, sharing feelings, laughing and crying together. Why not encourage your children to talk to God this same way? Help them express their true feelings and put a little life into their prayers. I'll guarantee that their relationship with God will grow. Here's how to begin:

TEACH YOUR CHILD TO BE A CREATIVE CONVERSATIONALIST

"Have you said your prayers yet?" one mom asked her seven year old as she bent over to kiss him good night.

"Well, not exactly," he replied. "I decided God must get pretty tired listening to the same old thing, so tonight I told Him the story of Goldilocks and the Three Bears."

Why not? I think my God would be pleased that we cared enough to share something with Him we thought He would really enjoy.

I wonder what God thinks when kids bow their heads and out tumble the same old memorized words, while their minds are on a baseball game or Susie's fancy dress? It's like saying mealtime grace by repeating the words, "Now I lay me down to sleep . . ." or blessing the food at bedtime. One little girl prayed, "God bless Bingo, Trixie, and . . ." without thinking she added, "Uncle Eddie has a farm E-I-E-I-O." When the child puts her mind in neutral and recites clichés, it's meaningless.

One night after my nine year old had prayed the same prayer each night for the last seven years, I asked, "Kevin, do you think God has ever heard that prayer before?"

"Yes," he admitted. "I prayed the same thing last night."

"Is that the only other time?"

"No," he smiled. "I prayed it the night before that, and the night before that, too."

"Kevin, do you tell your best friends the very same thing every day?"

"No, Mom. I tell them important things—like who won the soccer game and how to tie a square knot and why batteries go dead."

"Kevin, God is your very best friend. Don't you think He might like to hear something new—something that's really important—like the things you tell your best friends?"

"I don't know," said Kevin, shrugging his shoulders, "I never thought about that."

"God is interested in everything that happens to you," I continued, "and He wants to answer your prayers. You might not be able to hear Him, but you can think an answer and then continue talking. Just to give you an idea of what really talking to God is like, pray again and I'll answer what I think God might answer."

Kevin began again. "Dear God, I had a great time with Tim today."

I answered, "God might say to you, 'Kevin, I'm happy you did. Tell Me what you did together.' "

"Oh, we started building a tree house."

"That sounds like fun—and hard work."

"Yeah, it was hard work, but our tree house is safe. We braced the boards and jumped on them to make sure they wouldn't come loose."

"That was a good idea. What else did you do?"

Kevin continued his prayer. After about five minutes—which seemed like an eternity to me—I interjected, "Kevin, Mommy has worked hard all day, and I still have the dishes to do. Do you think we could say good night for now so I can get back to my work?"

"Sure," replied Kevin. "Talking to God is a lot more fun this way."

The next morning my husband asked Kevin to say grace. "Dear God," he began, "thank You for the good night's sleep—and for the terrific dream. I dreamed that we had a giant water slide in our backyard and a wave pool—a huge one just for me. It was just like the ocean. And I'm thankful we get to go to the zoo today. And please don't let me have to sit by a girl on the bus. And please help the myna bird to talk to me. And. . . ."

By this time the girls were fidgeting. If they didn't get the food blessed soon they would be late for school. "Kevin, the food—bless the food," Kim whispered.

Obviously, Kevin was enjoying his new relationship with God, and the girls did get to school on time. The few extra minutes it took to tell God about his dream and the field trip were well worth it. It perked up our usual morning routine—and I'm sure it made God smile.

TEACH YOUR CHILD TO TALK WITH GOD ABOUT WHAT IS ON HIS MIND AND HEART

God wants to hear about the headlines in our children's lives. And He wants to add His commentary, if a child will just talk with Him and not at Him.

Ask your child how he feels right now: bubbly all over, crabby, impish, discouraged, silly, ready to tackle the world, like his best friend has deserted him? Tell God about it. He's interested.

To help children tune in to their feelings, have sharing times during the day. Ask the question, "How are you feeling right now?" and then together kneel down and tell God about those feelings. Before jumping up, pause a minute, be quiet with God and listen for His reaction—the Holy Spirit speaking, making impressions on your mind. Ask your child, "What did God say?" and expect an answer.

One night six-year-old Kari and her older sister were wrestling and giggling instead of going to sleep as their dad had asked them to do. When I could stand it no longer I marched into their room like a general and commanded, "Stop immediately, or you're going to get it!" Quiet reigned.

Then I asked in a different tone of voice, "Have you girls said your prayers?" They knelt down and Kari prayed earnestly, "Dear Jesus, please help Mommy not to be so strict!" She said what was on her mind, and I helped God answer that prayer by apologizing for my behavior and tucking them gently into bed with a goodnight kiss.

TEACH YOUR CHILD TO PRAY FOR OTHERS

When Kevin was four he noticed a woman I knew in a neck brace and prayed, "Dear Jesus, please help the lady with the neck cast to get it off." I thought the prayer was cute and mentioned it to the woman. A couple of weeks later Kevin received a letter, "Dear Kevin. Since you prayed for me I haven't had to wear my neck brace. Thank you."

"God answered my prayer!" Kevin shouted as he danced around the room.

It is special when God answers a child's prayers and he gets a new bicycle, but nothing can match the joy a child experiences when God answers his prayers for someone else. Help your child make a prayer list. Encourage him to pray systematically for others; teach him to claim Bible promises for those in need; keep a prayer diary and remind your youngster to thank God for answers.

It won't take your child long to find a new friend in God when he begins talking creatively with Him, sharing what's really current in his thoughts or feelings and telling God about his other friends and loved ones. Why not encourage your child to have a little talk with God right now?

ENCOURAGE A PERSONAL EXPERIENCE WITH GOD

Inside-out character either grows or atrophies, depending on your child's relationship with God. The closer the relationship, the more Christlike the character. What can you do to help your child develop a personal experience with God?

1. Share your own experience with your child.

When children see parents having a dynamic relationship with God, it certainly makes it more appealing. Before World War II, My husband's father was a Protestant book salesman in Poland. As my husband, Jan, was growing up, he never doubted that God was real because of the miracle stories his father told him. For example, one winter day his father was being chased out of town by an angry mob. As he was running across a snowy field, suddenly he fell into a deep hole and was covered with snow. He wasn't able to crawl out until much later, after the mob had lost his tracks and were heading back to town. He was then able to continue home without harassment.

Can you imagine the impact on Jan and his brother and sisters when, day after day, these experiences were related to them? Surely this would be enough for Jan to have a good relationship with God. But it's not that simple. Vicarious experiences can never substitute for an experience in one's own life.

2. Help your child to step out in faith.

Unless a child is willing to step out in faith, he will really never know how much God is willing to do for him. Your child must have a personal experience. Jan lived through the terrible years of World War II. His father was taken away to a German labor camp, leaving his mother and four young children to manage on their own. Jan saw God provide food, shelter, and protection and, after the war, a means of crossing the communist border into the free world so the family could be reunited.

Are these childhood experiences enough to last a lifetime? No. A meaningful relationship with God must be maintained on a daily basis. But you can't expect God to work mighty miracles every day, can you? Of course you can. I'd say that keeping happy all day long is a mighty miracle. Or not losing your temper. Or being on time to every appointment.

Each one of us has different needs. If we just open these up to the Lord, it will give Him a chance to work mighty miracles each day, and we'll find our relationship with God growing closer. Encourage your child to ask in faith, and expect a miracle.

3. **Encourage your child to accept God's gift of salvation.**

As early as the child can comprehend, share with him the plan of salvation. A child doesn't have to be a twelve year old to understand that he is sinful, to ask God to forgive him, and to accept His gift of salvation. In fact, I believe the early school years, between seven and ten, are the years when a child is most open to God's salvation. When a child's heart is sensitive to

God's Spirit, don't wait for the pastor or for a more convenient time—you can be the one to lead your child to take this important step in his spiritual development.

When your child indicates that he accepts Jesus as his Savior, you can have him pray this prayer after you:

Dear Jesus,
I love You and want to be Your special child.
I am sorry for the wrong things I have done.
Forgive me for my sins.
And help me to obey You.
Thank You for dying on the cross for me.
I accept the gift of Your life. Thank You for saving me.
I love You.
Amen.

Once your child begins to experience God's power working in his life, he'll become more sensitive to the Holy Spirit, and you'll find him more willing to make decisions based on God's will as found in His Word. And the fruit? A beautiful inside-out character.

About the Author

Dr. Kay Kuzma is a noted child development specialist and author of more than a dozen books on parenting, including *Building Your Child's Character From the Inside Out*

Dr. Kuzma has appeared frequently on radio talk shows and on television programs such as NBC's *Today Show* and *Hour Magazine*. Kay and her husband, Jan, and their three children live in California.

HELPING FAMILIES GROW SERIES

❧ *Communicating Spiritual Values Through Christian Music*

❧ *Equipping Your Child for Spiritual Warfare*

❧ *Family Vacations that Work*

❧ *Helping Your Child Stand Up to Peer Pressure*

❧ *How to Discover Your Child's Unique Gifts*

❧ *How to Work With Your Child's Teachers*

❧ *Helping Your Child Love to Read*

❧ *Improving Your Child's Self-Image*

❧ *Preparing for Your New Baby*

❧ *Should My Child Listen to Rock Music?*

❧ *Spiritual Growth Begins At Home*

❧ *Surviving the Terrible Teenage Years*